My Barber and Me

By: Stephanie Sherer

Relentless Publishing House, LLC
Columbia, SC

RELENTLESS
PUBLISHING

My Barber and Me

Copyright © 2019 Stephanie Sherer

Published by:

Relentless Publishing House, LLC

www.relentlesspublishing.com

Printed in USA
First Printing: November 2019

ISBN: 978-1-948829-28-1

Dedication

This book was inspired by my brother, the master barber, Joel Battle, and my amazing son, Matthew. Being a part of the emotional moment where we as parents watched our little one get his first haircut was awe-inspiring. The fact that it was done by his uncle made it that much sweeter. The barbershop, much like the beauty shop, is about so much more than getting your haircut. It's a community staple, a shared cultural experience by all that participate. We hope you enjoy, as we take you through the journey. #wingz

My Barber and Me

I woke up this morning to a special treat. Mommy said, "It's time for you to go sit in the barber's seat."

This will be my first big haircut before the first day of school. I'm so excited! My dad and uncles have just been raving about it.

Daddy always comes home from the barbershop looking so cool. He told me, "Son, today's the big day to get your haircut for school."

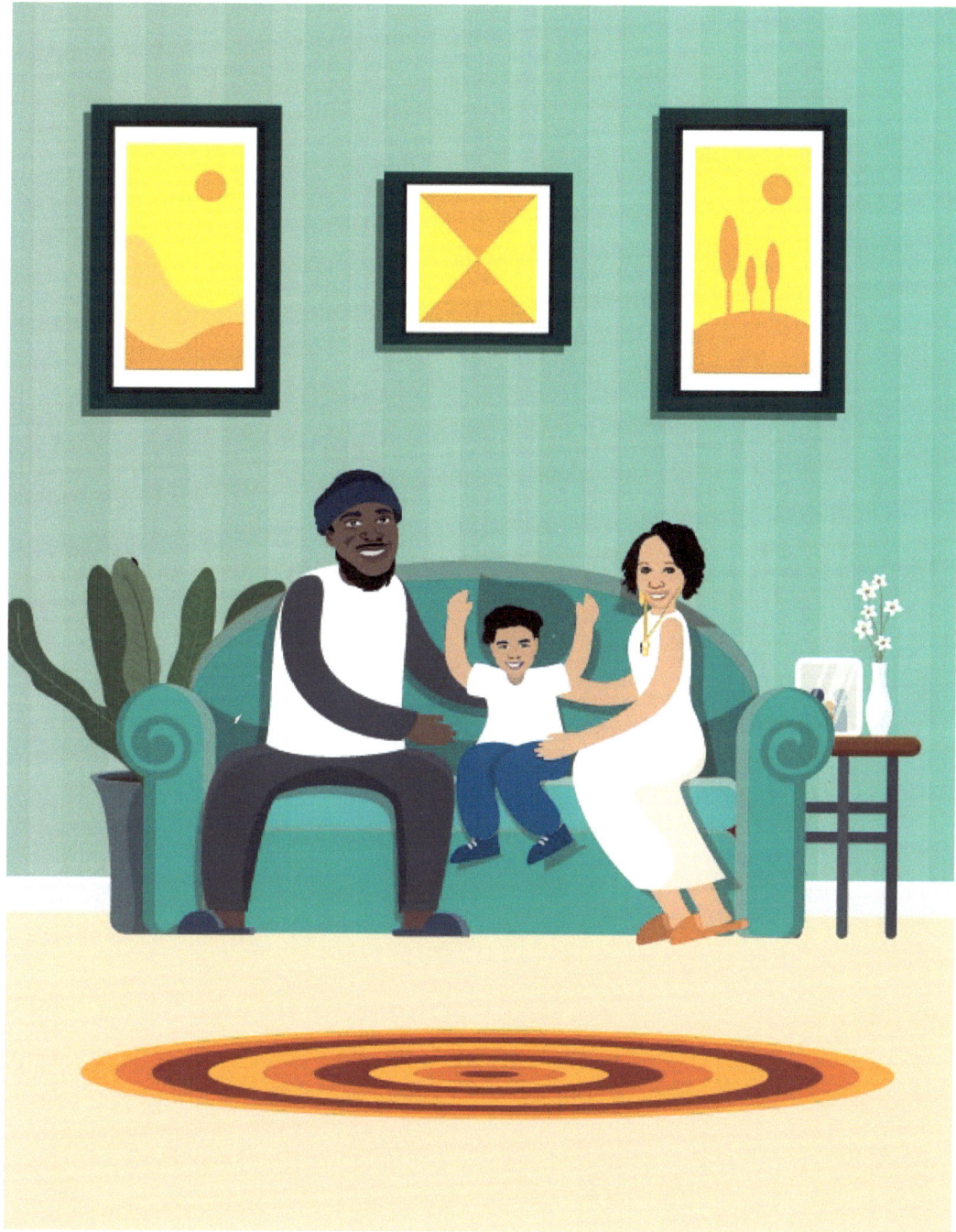

Now, don't get me wrong: I love my hair just the way it is. But I woke up ready for a change, so a haircut it is!

I had cereal with mommy to start the day, then we hopped in the car and were on our way.

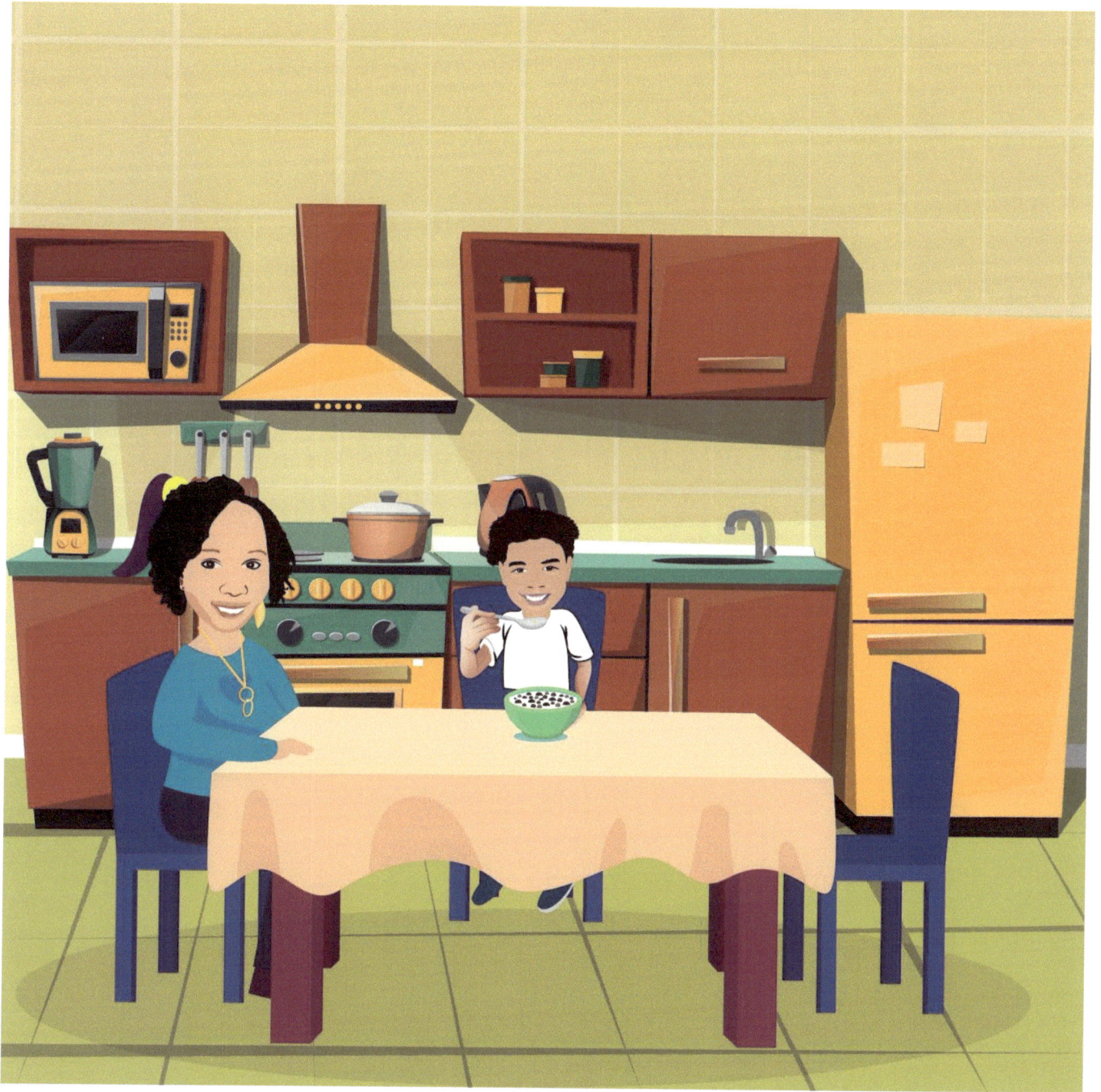

On the way to the shop, my dad said to me, "Son, before we walk into the shop, on one thing we must agree." "Yes dad," I said, smiling with glee.

"You see, the barbershop is a special place, where we gather to not only get haircuts, but also, to support one another. The barbershop will become a part of your village. It's a bond of brothers."

"I understand dad." I said, with an overwhelming sense of pride. The excitement I had about this special day, was a feeling I could not hide.

I walked in the shop, and my barber grinned and said, "My man, can I get a high-five?" I gave him a high five and hopped in his chair, thinking, "The day has come for me to finally cut my hair."

He wrapped a black cape around me, to protect my clothes from the hair. Then he cut on his clippers and told me to be still in the chair.

When he started to cut my hair, the clippers sounded and felt a little funny; The whole thing started to give me butterflies in my tummy.

My barber noticed me frowning, and told me to relax. He gave me a lollipop and said, "I'll be done in a flash."

As he continued to cut my hair, he spun my chair so I could see myself in the mirror. I began to think about my first day of school; my vision for success was becoming clearer.

In the mirror, I could see my mommy crying and my daddy grinning from ear to ear. "Why are you crying mommy," I asked. She said, "Son, these are happy tears."

My daddy said, "Getting haircuts at the barbershop are priceless moments, son. They are a rite of passage for every little one."

Next, my barber spun me around in the chair and said, "You're done my friend. You did a great job," while he shook my hand." "A smile and a haircut go a long way." Those are the words my barber left me with today.

As I hopped out of the seat, I was beaming with pride. I was ready to face the first day of school adventures with my fresh haircut and a smile I could not hide.

So, when the day comes for you, my friend, don't be afraid. The barbershop experience is one that you'll never want to trade.

About the Author

Stephanie Sherer is a passionate educator currently serving as a K-12 school counselor and independent college advisor. Her passions include social-emotional learning, literacy development and college access for all. *My Barber and Me* is her debut children's book.

www.ingramcontent.com/pod-product-compliance
Lightning Source LLC
Chambersburg PA
CBHW042120040426
42449CB00003B/127